KALECIANA PERRY

Why The Black Man Cries

The story of America unfolded, undecided by color and why we aren't one nation under God.

In Loving Memory of James Earl Chaney, and those who were slain, lynched, and beat just so I could be free, I say thank you.

Contents

Foreword

This book, *Why The Black Man Cries,* is powerful *alone* in its historical perspective, and history, of the Black experience in the United States. In addition, though, coupled with the truths and angers of our experience, the anger and outrage about these truths, are expressed by a 15 -year old. I am amazed at the fact, that such a young person has the ability to see through the untruths of America's freedom being available to *all* Americans, that this young person has the ability to speak knowledgeably about the repeated "broken promises" that have been made over generations, and that this young person has the ability to detail numerous examples of those promises throughout history. It makes this book both sad and amazing.

Kaleciana Gabrielle Perry's book lists, details and analyzes the problems with the lack of accountability of America towards her people. She provides details that travel back to slavery and that continue through to the present, in a well-thought out, well-expressed and well-written account.

As a College Professor, Author and one whose work involves interaction with youth at all ages, I find that Ms. Perry's book is both precocious and insightful. I urge potential readers to not prepare themselves to have an adventure with a 15-year old, but to see this as an adventure into the reality of the African American experience. This book is powerful!

I am uplifted by Kaleciana's knowledge and her ability to take that knowledge and write this book to both teach and enlighten others, as well as recognize, and impart, the importance and necessity of providing the information to others.

This book is a must read for African-Americans who are knowledgeable about their history, and particularly, and especially for our youth, and African Americans who are not particularly knowledgeable about their history. I highly recommend it.

Preston Love, Jr.
  Professor of Black Studies
  University of Nebraska at Omaha

Preface

Drafting this book was extremely difficult for me. Recounting everything that happened during slavery, and now, I forgot how to breathe. I'm not taking this as a funny matter, looking at pictures of black lynchings, and Supreme Court cases with unjust rulings, it hurt. I remember as a little girl, my mother made me watch *"12 Years a Slave,"* she told me that I was going to sit down and watch every bit of it. This movie moved me to tears, from the beatings, the rapes, and the lynchings of a mangled body left there lifeless on the tree. I stayed up that night and couldn't sleep, those were my people, who were my color, that died under the face of the white man. I knew that I couldn't sit here and be silent, I had to become the epitome of Dr. Martin Luther King Jr, I needed to fight. I read up on everything I could about my history, how it started and how it's happening as of now. I couldn't let what the white man done become a part of me. Days later, I prayed and ask God to give me words to speak and give me his hand in writing. I knew I was born to write, because every notebook that my mother owned, I took and wrote in it. Some days I'll be lying in bed, and the Holy Spirit speaks and gives me what to write, I knew then, that it was time for me to author a book. I had no idea of what it was going to be about, I just wrote, and it all fell into place. But, my gift of writing isn't to be kept for myself, it's to be given for those who are unable to speak, because they are silenced. I hope

I speak for all of us when I say, Black Lives Matter, and we do stand with you.

Kaleciana Perry.

Acknowledgement

I want to thank God first for giving me the ability to make this book. Finally, I want to acknowledge everyone who helped make this book possible. My deepest gratitude to all of you.

Picture Use

I have used all pictures with permission by the declaration of the owner. It does not allow these pictures to be used unless given consent by the owner from which they came. All pictures from sites are credible.

I

America's Slave System From The Beginning

You read correctly, from the beginning.

1

The Negro

"Being a Negro in America means trying to smile when you want to cry. It means trying to hold on to physical life amid psychological death. It means the pain of watching your children grow up with clouds of inferiority in their mental skies. It means having your legs cut off, and then being condemned for being a cripple. It means seeing your mother and father spiritually murdered by the slings and arrows of daily exploitation, and then being hated for being an orphan."
-Quote by Dr. Martin Luther King Jr.

2

The Cry of King, Unfulfilled

50 years later, a man who had made a difference with his dream, shattered. If Dr. King was alive today, what would he say? That the shame of our nations has fallen in the palms of the man who thought he was bigger than himself. That people were supposed to come together and stand unified as one, but we use bullets to fight instead of our hearts. We use words to kill, but not our actions. You say that we fight, but for what reason? Why are you skimming over the meat? Get down to the bone where the flavor is and see what I see. Dr. King fought for the resilience of this country and gave us life. He died for you selfish people, and here you are, standing here with your face turned to the wall, asking, why me? Well, why not you, what happened to "keep the faith?," or "faith is taking the first step even when you don't see the whole staircase?" You forgot about that. Children look into their eyes of their mother and wonder, "Mama, will we be okay?" "I don't know baby, only God knows the fate of his people." What about the little boy holding hands with his sister in the classroom's corner, texting his family his last goodbye, "I love you, Mama." And then pow, nothing left. Will the death

of my people become my new name? Or will it just remain the same? Therefore, I fight if no one will carry the torch to continue the legacy. I fight for you because Dr. King fought for me.

3

A Separate Nation

"One nation under God, indivisible with Liberty and Justice for all" sounds familiar. The ending of the Pledge is supposed to grant Liberty and Justice to all. Well, "all" is only for the white man; black people have never received justice for anything. Miles and miles away from freedom that was never granted.

America, ask yourself this question: Are we one nation under God? America, you aren't a nation under God. God isn't white; God is a spirit.

God made everyone from black dirt; it is because of the nutrients in black soil that make it constructive; therefore, black soil is the richest soil there is. It has more nutrients than any other color soil. We are all the same, but you can't see that. You elected a former president who wasn't worth two nickels, and now America is bringing slavery back. God never created the white man; you aren't white America; you're black. We always say, "God bless America," God doesn't need to bless America; he needs to bless you too.

Through the time of slavery and race riots in America, white people have become the epitome of ignorance. Some white people, not all. In slave times, your enslavers grew up with privilege; they had everything planned for them. Otherwise, for blacks, we were pushed into the gutter, clinging to our lives while being beaten. No, America, you know what you have done. You took advantage of us in every way. When black men were lynched, you stood and laughed your way into a coma. With your harrowing stories of how white people got away with murdering black people.

Everywhere you go, racism is lurking at the door. There will not be one place you go where you aren't discriminated against. They watch us like hawks, as if you stole a piece of their life.

They must teach racism for one to become racist, because the apple doesn't fall far from the tree. If racism surrounds you, your mind will develop those habits and fall right into the hole. That may not be the case for everyone, but it makes up for many of America's problems today.

You don't just wake up one morning and become a racist. It doesn't matter if there were "ancient theories of racism," racism has been around ever since God created the Earth, even in Biblical times. Racism affects how we see the world today; we will never know how racism started or how we can end it. We filled the world with incompetent people. No matter where you look, racism will be the founder of this country.

This is the place we live in, the area that we call home. We aren't together as one, but your flesh under one individual.

4

The Beginning of Slavery

Slavery has been around beyond the 17th and 18th centuries; It was the first time it grew. They kidnapped people from Africa.

We know this continent as the "Mother Continent." Our ancestors have lived in Africa for over 6 million years. What was the purpose? Africa comprises black people, Aborigines, Haitians, and others. All of them originated from Africa. You, as people, come from Africa. The most dedicated people were from Mother Countries. They knew everything about working, cooking, and sewing. After the Reconstruction Era, wars angered white (pale pink) people and ongoing history from the past. Therefore, black people were taken from their homes and worked as dogs. Due to black people having an advantage in working, white people took over these countries. They knew black people were skilled in everything they did; that's what white people wanted; they needed to take control of the other race and break them. Amid their eyes, they had total control.

The economy was rebuilt during the Reconstruction Era. Instead, people started using black people, and taking control of how they were viewed.

Lynching, incest, sexual assault, beatings, skinning, decapitating their heads, and putting them on the front door to see what they had carried out.

Even though lynching was just one of the cruel punishments, slavery expanded. The call for abolition of slavery was far away in the North. Raids began, and abolitionists came out of the open. The revolutionary war acknowledged slavery,

"counting each enslaved individual as three-fifths of a person for taxation and representation in Congress and guaranteeing the right to repossess any "person held to service or labor" (an obvious euphemism for slavery).[1]

There were many ways black people could be enslaved.

1. Being kidnapped was the fundamental way Europeans would raid African huts and villages.
2. Enslaved black people had iron necks and muzzles around them, with chains linked to their ankles and hands to keep them from running away.
3. Slavery in ancient times wasn't primarily based on race, but as a debt, Prisoner of War, or punishment for crime.
4. Sometimes, Kings and Chiefs would sell black people for goods in European countries.

There were many passages and states of trade.

---

[1] Slavery in America." *History*, A&E Television Networks, 12 Nov. 2009, www.history.com/topics/black-history/slavery. Accessed 3 Feb. 2023.

1. The Outward Passage: Traded goods from Europe to Africa to receive more slaves.
2. The Middle Passage: Black people were taken and shipped across the Atlantic Ocean.
3. Inward Passage: Trades of sugar and tobacco to Europe.

Out of all the passages that followed the Slave Trade, the Middle Passage was the most gruesome. They crammed black men below the ship's deck while being handcuffed around their ankles and wrists. The deck wasn't high enough for anyone to stand. Making curvatures in their backs while sitting for an extended period. The journey of the Middle Passage lasted for seven weeks, and black people were allowed outside twice a day. Because of the constant filth on the ship (purposefully set up this way), many black people suffered from diseases such as dysentery, smallpox, and drapetomania (this was known as the disease that makes "negroes" escape. Samuel Cartwright emphasized this in his hypothesis of mental illness in 1851. Which, in this case, if you were kept in captivity by a "Massa" you would feel the same thing our ancestors did.)

Out of nearly 13 million slaves traveling on the Middle Passage, it is estimated that only 11 million survived. This started with the Portuguese in 1440, when they transported black people to America through the Middle Passage. As of 1619, the first twenty black people arrive as slaves or laborers without freedom from the Kingdom of Hdongo.

Each year, the number progressed of enslaved black people, soars to the millions.

1720-1869: 6,150,000 slaves were estimated through the years of an upward tick.

Slavery has become a source of money, and racist involvement has grown across the globe. Now, all black people are being held under duress as we demand what belongs to us and our ancestors. Slavery never started in America; it started in foreign countries by people who wanted power over others. Learn something sometime. It might just help you throughout your life.

5

The Clay Covered Man with a Touch of Pink

The Black Pharaohs of Egypt are a crucial example of slavery. Back then, black Pharaohs owned slaves, and in this era, it wasn't about color among people or different entities; it was about who had the most power and how they would rule. One of the first African Pharaohs was King Piankhi; he was the first to rule Egypt from 730 to 656 BC. He was also the founder of the 25th dynasty; this dynasty was the final part of the Third Intermediate Period, categorized as the Nubian Invasion that occurred after. The 25th dynasty was a new beginning for Egypt along with Kush; it brought new strength and reunion, among others. But, also with this, a war began to spark; with war comes power, and with power comes the need, and need becomes enslaving others for the awakening attack. Ramses II owned Nubian slaves during the new temples' production. Today, we often think about Ramses being a Caucasian man, but the term Caucasian from the Oxford dictionary is "white-skinned, or of European origin." If you do your research correctly, you will find out that Europeans are NOT white; they are fully black. When God created man, he created him from the richest dirt on Earth, which was black dirt; therefore, the Mississippi Delta has the most fertilized soil; black dirt is good for gardening because of the nutrients and thickness of the dirt, this gives its part for shaping and molding.

White wasn't a term until 1775; it was used as a weapon of white supremacy to demonize and uplift white people. The reason we have these assorted colors of skin is due to the melanin of the skin, causing all black people's skin color to be what it is. The term Caucasian came from Russia because Russians aren't white. Russians come from Eastern Europe, and early ancestors of Europe were black, and the ancestors of Russians came from Slavic Tribes, "As a result the Slavic tribes were divided into three branches - southern, western and eastern. The eastern Slavs are the ancestors of the modern Russians." Here's the part that breaks it all, "From Middle English, from Old French sclave, from Medieval Latin sclāvus ("slave"), from Late Latin Sclāvus ("Slav"), because **Slavs were often forced into slavery in the Middle Ages.**" [2]

In today's world, we see that it has revolved around "color." In Biblical times, different tribes made up the nation's populations back then. But, during the 15th Century and beyond, "color" began to take place. To deepen your understanding of what I am addressing, let's begin with the Book of Genesis:

We can see that God created man in his image. God made Adam from the dust of the Earth (the dust is black, not white).

---

[2] Mair, Victor. "Slavs and Slaves." *Languagelog*, 17 Jan. 2019, languagelog.ldc.upenn.edu/nll/?p=41445. Accessed Feb. 2023.

The word Adam means "Son of the red Earth." The bloodstream comes from him, so all of us are descendants of Adam and Eve because the human race started with them. Furthermore, God makes Eve from Adam's rib cage. This is why we have the term "DNA," the curve of the rib is the same cure as the "Helix Curve." In this case, since ribs are made of cartilage, Adam did not go his entire life without his rib, it eventually grew back.

So far, we have established that Adam and Eve are both black from the contents from which they were made. Nowhere in the Bible is there a single white person. Every ideology linked to Jesus' birth and beyond, all persons for an account were Black. After the flood, Noah's children Shem, Ham, and Japheth, left their land and integrated, married, and then consequently, they had mixed children. In depictions of Ancient hieroglyphics and drawings, we see that every last painting has black people on it.

Ancient Painting From Africa (Egypt)

Picture. [3]

There is your answer, everybody on this Earth has black ancestry leading to the beginning of the Earth's creation. Adam and Eve were the first black people on this Earth. We are all related to each other because we come from the first humans. "God did not create any more humans in the way He had created them, and He gave them the command to "be fruitful and multiply and fill the earth" (Genesis 1:28). All other humans came from those first parents, so in that sense, we are all related to each other." [4]

_____

[3] "The Curse of Black Skin." *Deuteronomy 26*, www.deuteronomy28.org/black-skin.html.
     Accessed 13 Dec. 2022.

[4] "Are We Are Related?" *Got Questions*, www.gotquestions.org/are-we-all-related.html. Accessed 3 Feb. 2023.

Does God Accept Slavery?

The answer is no he does not accept it. In the Bible, if a man were to commit a crime, he would have to pay the debt by working. Slavery in biblical time was not perpetual, which means it didn't exceed to generations. What people don't realize about slavery is that, in the Bible slavery wasn't based on race, it was based on crime committed. Rather, as of now, it's about black people. It is from the pigmentation in our skin that our parents DNA gives us, the "white term," and "black term." God created only one race because he knew we as people would kill each other over what we look like.

I will simplify this by saying that "black", which is not necessarily "jet black" but rather dark-skin, is *the only skin-color* that can produce the full range of colors from "white" to "black". Neither "medium" skin, nor "white" skin can do the same in and of themselves. All nations of color, from "black" to "medium" produce "white" offspring in the form of albinos. "White" nations generally do not produce "medium", and sure enough do not produce "black" offspring.[5]

"But rather dark-skin, is *the only skin-color* that can produce the full range of colors from "white" to "black." Here's the kicker, we get white from black, which means the beginning human race on Earth was black, meaning if white comes from black, we as people of the United States of America are all black. Because black is the only color capable of producing these high

---

[5] "Were Noah's Three Sons Three Different Colors?" *Wake-up Israelites*, 9 Oct. 2011, wakeupisraelites.wordpress.com/2011/10/09/ were-noahs-three-sons-three-different-colors/. Accessed 3 Feb. 2023.

pigmentation to get "white." So you white you see is really just the color black.

It's funny, how we kill each other, and that our own race turns against itself. Look at Tyre Nichols, beaten to death by 5 black police officers who look just like him. Why? What is the point for all of this hate? We are all related and this is how we treat one another. It's shameful. We, as people, will not stand for long, killing your own family, and walking away.

Know who you are; when you die, your color won't matter, but who you were as a person and what you did will be the response.

6

Racism in Biblical Times

You can have your feelings of racism and slavery, from where it occurred and why. Racism has appeared throughout Biblical times, from the beginning of Noah's Flood and after. In the book of Exodus, the Israelites were put into slavery by Pharaoh; scholars say that Pharaoh was known as Ramses II. The Israelites multiplied greatly in Egypt, and Pharaoh feared the people before him. God sent multiple plagues among Pharaoh, telling him if he didn't let God's people go, the punishment was coming among Pharaoh's land, and so it did; God sent the 10 Plagues on Egypt.

Water turning to blood, frogs, lice, flies, livestock pestilence, boils, hail, locusts, darkness, and the killing of firstborn children.

Out of all the plaques, the locusts were the deadliest. When locusts fly together, they start to become gregarious. In this case, there were so many locusts that you couldn't see the land ahead. They ate up all the vegetation and left nothing behind.

There are many more biblical encounters with slavery. God freed his people by parting the Red Sea; it wasn't Moses who parted it. God gave Moses the staff to stretch over the sea, but God drove the sea back by an east wind. For instance, God did any means necessary to free the Israelites from slavery from the beginning of the Exodus unto the end.

This should be how the people of America fight, never giving up until all people have received justice. If that means pushing people out of the way to get what we want, so be it. Galatians 3:28 says that; "There is neither Jew nor Greek, slave nor free, male nor female, for you are all one in Christ Jesus." If God can love us all for who we are, then we need to follow in his footsteps. That means leaving your smart mouth remarks about each other in the gutter. Because if we want to truly move forward as a nation under God, you need to start acting like it. Equality comes from treating everyone as human, and leading in love not hate. Understanding that we are all to blame for this nations downfall, and most importantly, understanding that not all consequences come automatically, but one voice will rain and all inequality will cease. If we want to love one another, we need to shed the same tears of pain, just like the black man did when all of his people were lynched. The tears he shed were not only for the remorse of his family, but for us because he knew we would feel the same type of pain. To know the world we live in, defines not only our flesh, but the attributes of who we are, really does say something on how we view each other daily. We need to take a good look in the mirror and ask ourselves, "Am I fighting for a better tomorrow, or waiting for time to stand still?" It's horrible to see this nation fight over skin color, how petty can you be to fight and kill us because of what we look like. But, I will make this perfectly clear, if God could wipe out a sinful nation with a flood, what do you think he will do with us. Reevaluate your choices before you become the one going up a stream without a boat, in other words, before you fight, you need to be equipped not for the war, but for what comes after it.

"And the glory of the Lord shall be revealed, and all flesh shall see it together" (Isaiah 40:5 -8).

Through the Israelites' oppression, and heartache, God fought for their freedom; we need to be uprooted in what is happening now. "You can lead a horse to water, but you can't make him drink." We may not be able to end racism, but we can get people to listen. Not with guns, protests, or killings. You have a mouth; use it. You are put on Earth for a purpose, fight for what is right, and stand up against the wrong. The time has come to fight. You either fight for what's right, or become caught in the rapture like the rest of this nation.

II

The Political Outcry

The Journey of black people across health and wellness and climbing up the wall to a greater calling. Here you will find the contrast between America through biblical relations and why this nation is emotionally and politically dead.

The Nations downfall.

7

I Pray, You Pray, We Pray

Prayer shouldn't be overlooked from a historical standpoint. In slave times, black people prayed to God for freedom. In fact, Martin Luther King Jr's famous speech "I have a dream" was a prayer-based inspiration that captured the attention of those there to hear him. Using biblical scriptures, King emphasized the importance of unity and ending the separation of brotherhood.

At that time, white masters believed God was white; they felt God wasn't for black people. Prayer has always become sacred from a public and private standpoint. White enslavers would come into churches and bomb them just because black people were together, and whites didn't understand their "sort of language."

The 16th Street Baptist Church was bombed on September 15, 1963, in Birmingham, Alabama. A white terrorist group (Ku Klux Klan) attacked this church as it killed four black girls. The four girls, three of them being fourteen, were Addie Mae Collins, Denise McNair, Carole Robertson, and eleven-year-old Cynthia Wesley. The bombing happened under the church stairwell, while people inside the church shielded each other from debris.

16th street Baptist Church. Known as "Black Jesus" to some. One hand is pushing out racism and oppression, while the other hand is bringing in unity. The arrow is going to his heart, this stands for the pain of slavery and white supremacy on black people. The picture can be interpreted either way. This stained-glass mural was made by John Petts, he read what happened and offered his services in honor of the four victims.

After this incident and after hearing of the aftermath, Martin

Luther King Jr wrote a telegram to George Wallace, an idiotic psychopath who abused his power for self-victory. King said in this telegram to Wallace "The blood of our little children is on your hands." In this case, it was; Wallace couldn't see behind his disgusting and blemishing ways as a sick governor.

Prayer in slave times was the only way to protect themselves. If you were a black person caught with a gun, you were shot dead in the street. Caught trying to escape, your body was mutilated and often left out to decay. This was and still is America.

Black people would listen to different preachers of their choice without their slaveholder's knowledge. In this, they would pray for unity, the breaking of their chains, and the downfall of racism. This is how the term "Invisible Church" came along.

Through prayer, black people were free. Free from bondage, and free from constant staples in the road. Prayer was a gift from those who received it, and they would rejoice when God heard their prayers.

I understand you may think politics and religion have nothing to do with each other.
    Then why do you have "God Bless America" as your motto?

Prayer is what America needs right now; with all the revelations that were seen and experienced back then, we can learn a lot from our ancestors. Prayer was their ultimate way of escaping life itself.

Their prayer needs to be our prayer today.

Lord, save us from the coming back of slavery.

Black people won't be able to vote or even have freedom. Segregation will be the significant setback America will face because in the end, whose report will you believe?

8

Dream Chaser

The situations that have happened are just the beginning of what's to come. Black history is and should be important to all black people. But, as the Gen Z generation grows up, how will they know that these events happened and why they took place? Nowadays, our black children hardly ever want to come to school, and when they do, they are targeted for showing up.

America has made so many statistics on black people that it has become a trend among all white people. Research states that:

Black and African American student borrowers are the most likely to struggle financially due to student loan debt, with 29% making monthly payments of $350 or more.[6]

Money shouldn't have to be a problem to chase your dreams;

---

[6] Hanson, Melanie. "Student Loan Debt by Race" EducationData.org, June 13, 2022,
https://educationdata.org/student-loan-debt-by-race

this is one of the most outstanding issues America is facing. Aid must be available to everyone, no matter their color because it's something we all do. We dream.

While America spends its money on the economy, taxes, and legislation bills, you have more white people in more dominating jobs. They come from wealthier backgrounds (some, not all). If you were to ask what a black child wanted to be when they grew up. It's either:
 "I have to stay home and help my parents."
 Or
 "I can't afford it; dreams don't pay the bills."

Dreams pay the bills; when you become your dream, you live the dream. Why don't you give black children the opportunity to pursue theirs?
Needless to say, on the topic of dreams, the American Dream is a fraud. Oxford dictionary calls the American Dream.
 "The ideal by which equality of opportunity is available to any American, allowing the highest aspirations and goals to be achieved."

"Available to any American," yes, any American that is white, not colored. Consequently, Francis Scott Key was an enslaver who made the National Anthem which was a poem. Ironically, "the land of the free" only applied to white primaries who had the freedom to hold enslaved people; no freedom was applied to black people. America has never believed in equality or liberty. The American Dream is what it is, a dream, a lie, a fascist part of this government. Therefore, protesters took down the Francis Scott Key statue, Key was a part of the American Dream, but he just made it harder for us—enslaving people and ostracizing the blackness. There's no point in chasing the American Dream; the laws America has given permit us from even living. We aren't the land of the free, and instead, we are living in a world that revolves around the white man.

It is no surprise how the white man took black people's ideas. My ancestors worked hard to give me a better life so I could be free. But all that is just to be thrown away because of their color. Their stories will never be forgotten, and neither will this one:

Nathan Green was in Tennessee in the 1820s. Green was an expert distiller behind the famous brand Jack Daniels. Green helped Daniels with the whiskey and the understanding of the business. Daniels then used Green's recipe and put his name on it. So, the so-called "Jack Daniels" brand you buy is Green's whiskey. Furthermore, since Green was enslaved, Daniels took advantage of that because he was black.

Even through all of this, black people were the very ones who made the most significant inventions that would forever shape our future as we live.

Fredrick M. Jones- Air conditioning unit
  G. Cook- Auto fishing device
  Richard B. Spikes- Auto gear shift
  Charles Drew- Blood plasma bag
  Henry T. Sampson- Cellular car phone
  Alexander Miles- Elevator
  Lydia D. Newman- Hair brush

Madam CJ Walker- Straightening comb
Joseph N. Jackson- TV remote control
Garrett Morgan- Traffic light

Black people have done more for our future than any other man on this Earth. These brilliant minds had a time and place for everything they invented. It's no wonder all our efficient appliances come from intelligent black women and men.

Furthermore, how can we cherish these stories if they aren't taught in school? How can our black children grow up knowing how the past centuries have shaped us as one?

This is now the ground we stand on, don't leave its history behind. The American dream and your dream are no match and will never be. America is only here for self-gain, not to see you shine.

9

Systemic Racism

T here are many broad approaches to racism. Explicitly speaking, voting rights. Even though the 13th Amendment freed enslaved people, this didn't grant black people the right to vote. Across states, after enslaved black people were "free," whites didn't want black people to vote. That is why literacy tests, poll taxes, fraud, and intimidation were used. Here's an explanation of how these worked:

Literacy tests: For a black person to "vote," they had to take a literacy test. You had to get all the questions correct to pass the test. Knowing that black people were in captivity, they never learned how to read, so using this test took advantage of them.

Literacy tests were a swindle; even if a black person got every question right, they were still unable to vote. The literacy test was purposely made for black people to fail.

The shame black people went through to vote in the South was horrendous. It was either: you don't vote, or you vote and face the county sheriff who loads his gun in front of you, killing you before you can vote.

Under the circumstances, if a black person did vote, that individual would be hung for everyone to pass by and see, with the sign on his back:

"This nigger voted."

This was called the Grandfather Clause; it kept black slave descendants from voting. The clause states that you couldn't vote unless your grandfather voted.

These situations have been debated in Congress, but no response or action was regulated. Many amendments were passed, but each of them did absolutely nothing.

The 13th Amendment- abolished slavery in all U.S states.

This Amendment freed enslaved people, but police brutality is still slavery, killing off black people just for the joy of it. Even after the Amendment was passed, black people were enslaved, not under the need but political power. Also, the 13th Amendment clearly says that "involuntary servitude, except as punishment," this exception meant that if a black person was trying to pay off a debt, he was still considered a slave, in other words it makes up slavery. So, nothing has freed or abolished slavery.

14th Amendment- granted equal and legal rights to black people. (This is a lie from hell). From the time of slavery until now, no equality has been shown, no justice or granted promises for the things we've been owed.

15th Amendment- Guaranteed black men the right to vote.

33

This is still a lie; in most countries, they are trying to make strict political laws against black people, so they won't be able to vote. Voter suppression is not only taking over black communities; it's becoming a part of the constitution. They want you to fail at everything you do. America's system is corrupt.

Life is going to get much more challenging from here; it's going to become worse. The world is slowly becoming a spiral down-fall. "Injustice anywhere is a threat to justice everywhere." - Dr. Martin Luther King Jr.

10

Chains

C hains in slave times not only humiliated enslaved people, but slaveholders saw submission while they chained enslaved people. They saw us cry out every time the whip hit our backs, the stinging pain with every lash. White people laughed; they thought the pain we experienced was funny in their eyes. Nevertheless, the chains prevented us from walking or running away.

The adaptation of Alex Haley's Roots. Kunta Kinte was an enslaved man who tried to run away multiple times. On this offense, Kunta was caught by two slave catchers. The slave catchers gave Kunta a choice: either being castrated or having the front of his right foot cut off with an ax. For the rest of the scene, as Kunta had his foot cut off, the people in the crowd shook their heads in agreement.

White people thought having superiority over the black race was the key to power, making us feel like we don't belong. The soil of America is and always will be the black foundation. When the song Shackles by Mary Mary came out, it was more than the spiritual binding of Satan; it stood for the phenomenon of black people becoming free and resting in the Almighty. The Black Churches proved its long meaning of testimonies, all black people would say when they were freed, "Free at last, free at last, thank God Almighty, I'm free at last."

Even though the white man put iron muzzles on enslaved people to prevent them from eating, collars with bells to deter the escaping of enslaved people, lynching posters on trees if enslaved people were found, and constant darkness for enslaved people. But no longer will the duress of America bring strongholds; we will build our own country that will indeed be the "Land of the Free."

The chains that will be broken fall to the ground on the new soil built. In the future, a baby will lay with a lion, and the lion will not harm it. Just as so, a new tomorrow will come, where America will truly see the glory of its people. Go out and live the dream Martin Luther King Jr once had because you are the dream.

11

Boston Massacre of 1770

U nfortunately, this was just one of the many massacres to come. The Boston Massacre occurred on March 5th, 1770, in Boston, which took place on King Street. The brawl was between the American colonists and the British. Before this time, colonists rebelled against the taxes Britain tried to enforce. Therefore, the slogan by Patrick Henry, "No taxation without representation," came along due to the Stamp Act that was strong in Massachusetts.

Tensions rose and escalated quickly; on February 22nd, patriots attacked a loyalist's store. Ebenezer Richardson tried to break up the fight, but amidst gunfire, the crowd fired a shot through the window and hit an 11-year-old boy named Christopher Seider. Outraged patriots were engulfed with anger. More fights broke out between workers in stores; even though there was no bloodshed, the incident that was about to come was more significant than what had happened.

At this moment, on the same day, a clique of nine British soldiers went ahead to shoot five people in a crowd of four hundred. Around nine o'clock, a group of men shot and killed Crispus Attucks, an unarmed black man. The group of men who got away with this massacre was more than just a political motivator; it reflects the specific problems people face when different beliefs come in contact.

This massacre became the turning point for American soil; it increased colonists and taxation, which was unfair. This was another reason to fight for independence where they lived. Just as we do for a better tomorrow.

12

Bleeding Kansas

R ace riots and wars were the critical points to solving problems during slavery. Whether it be killing some ten hundred black men or lynching them as a symbol of power, this war isn't what you think. Bleeding Kansas was a guerrilla war between pro-slavery and anti-slavery; this political war started the coming of the Civil War. More than fifty-five people were killed in this period between 1855 and 1859.

The man behind this was none other than John Brown. This man was white (pale pink) but stood up for the rights of black people. In this time, if a white man protected enslaved people, he was called the n-word, along with a warrant for his arrest. The same example shows up in the 2017 movie "Marshall." Sam Friedman was brutally beaten and called out by two white men who called him the n-word because he was standing for Joseph Spell (the man who was accused of sexually assaulting his boss Eleanor Strubing).

Brown and his team began to march through Pottawatomie Valley in Kansas. On May 24th, 1856, John and his members planned the murder of settlers who wanted to keep slavery and favored it. At this moment, the night of May 24th, John, his group of seven men, and his four sons attacked five pro-slavery men in their homes. After that, a series of violent confrontations broke out (all because of a debate over slavery proposed in Kansas).

Pro-slavery white men couldn't stand it if anti-slavery people won the debate over slavery; they needed their "property" to be with them simply because they took their anger out on black people. This was just one way they tried to succeed. Unfortunately, Brown's raid failed, and he was later executed and martyred among those seeking justice for slavery, trying to make it the official end to another war. John Brown was the first man to be martyred with treason in the United States on December 2nd, 1859.

Raid On Harper's Ferry, John Brown Part II

John Brown, a slave abolitionist (as said above), and twenty-two men, five black, began a raid on pro-slavery activists. This occurred from October 16th to the 18th of 1859; this started a slave revolt in many southern states. Among this, it resulted in the death of ten people.

Harpers Ferry is a town in West Virginia. Located there is Ferry National Park and John Brown's Fort. This major raid was supposed to be the first stage in a plan to diminish the oppression of enslaved people and free them. If this raid had succeeded, the second stages of Brown's movement would be ongoing throughout. This would free enslaved people in the mountain regions such as Maryland and Virginia.

Slavery abolitionists agreed to take this militant cause to end the oppression of slavery. People may have died from this war, but this has a deeper meaning.

We can't hate white people, no matter how badly they treated us. Back then, there were some excellent white men in significance. A white man helped Harriet Tubman on the Underground Railroad; his name was Thomas Garrett. In this war, Brown was another man with a different story. In the North, Brown was proclaimed a "martyred hero" instead; in the South, he was a mass murderer.

Yes, the first lesson of black history you learned in school was Martin Luther King Jr, Malcolm X, Rosa Parks, Harriet Tubman, Fredrick Douglass, and all these masterminds. Have you come to reckon there were more people out there fighting for your freedom?

People like:

Harriet Beecher Stowe: authored a book called *Uncle Tom's Cabin*. She writes about the horrific experiences of black people as enslaved people in the United States.

Paul Cuffee: Fought to help give African and Native Americans the right to vote.

William Howard Day: Lobbied for the official boycott of cotton as it was human-led bondage.

Josiah Henson, Paul Jennings, Robert Morris, John Mercer Langston, Solomon Northup, Sarah Parker Remond, Marry Ann

Shadd, and many more.

These rebellions led to the importance of why black history is essential to the mouths of young people. Its history feeds your soul, and it hungers for more.

If there was someone who fought for you during slave times, and you could meet them if they were alive, who would you thank? It's time to rise from resentment and look beyond words because talk is cheap, but it takes money to buy land.

13

The Black Exodus of 1879

This movement began in the mid-1870s. Through the fight for Reconstruction, black people decided to leave the Southern countries in hopes of finding equal rights on the western frontier. The book of Exodus is where black people came up with the name "Exodusters."

In a letter to the 2nd Congressional District, black people wrote the reason for choosing to migrate to Kansas.

August 1, 1879

We the people of the 2nd Congressional District, North Carolina, have a Strong Desire to Emigrate to Kanses Land Where we can Have a Home. Reason and why:

1. We have not our rights in law.
2. The old former masters do not allow us anything for our labor.
3. We have not our Right in the Election. We are defrauded by our former masters.

4. We have not no [right] to make an honest and humble living.

5. There is no use for the Colored to go to law after their Rights; not one out of 50 gets his Rights.

6. The Ku [Klux Klan] Reigns.

7. We Want to Get to a land Where we can Vote and it not be a Crime to the Colored Voters.

8. Wages is very low [here]

Nearly all of the laborers have families to take care of and many other things we could mention, but by the help of God, we intend to make our start on Kansas land. We had Rather Suffer and be free than to suffer [the] infamous degrades that are Brought upon us" [here] 2

Rev. S Heath

Moses Heath

Lenoir Co., N.C.[7]

The Exodus of 1879 helped move 6,000 black people from various places such as Mississippi, Louisiana, and others. The goal of this mission was freedom, land, and prosperity. With such a mission as this, problems would arise. Currently, this movement was the very first migration following the Civil War. After the Reconstruction Era had ended, white people kept blacks from being free, using political disenfranchisement to subjugate African Americans and undo their gains during Reconstruction. This meant passing a law called Black Codes. This law restricted blacks from owning, prospering, leasing

---

[7] S. Heath and Moses Heath, "Black "Exodusters" Explain their Reasons for Leaving the South," *SHEC: Resources for Teachers*, accessed December 12, 2022, https://shec.ashp.cuny.edu/items/show/682.

land, and moving to other places.

The whole goal of the Exodusters was to migrate to Kansas and embark on unfamiliar territory for freedom. In everything blacks did to free their people, political demands on killing the race were to follow. Passing laws to prohibit the further activity of black people's freedom. The white Southerners tried to stop blacks from reaching Kansas and again used violent arrangements to keep them from being free. Even though whites were trying to stop them, black people kept going. Throughout the decade of the 1870s, Kansas's population rose to over 26,000 people.

This movement caused a dramatic change for all black people, even today. If it wasn't for our ancestors fighting behind closed doors, "free" would have never been added to "freedom," or it wouldn't have been a word at all.

14

Declaration of Independence

You may think that the Declaration of Independence was important because it made the United States an independent country from Great Britain. Truth is, it's not a big deal; it's fake. While the United States was an independent country, at the time of the signing, Thomas Jefferson, one of the authors of the Declaration of Independence, owned over six hundred enslaved people; this was the most of any U.S president ever. The Declaration states, "Life, Liberty, and the pursuit of Happiness." This wasn't for black people at all. Instead, it asserts that black people have no life, liberty, and happiness according to the law.

During slavery, you were emotionally dead from white people's verbal and derogatory images. Jefferson enslaved people all his life; he called slavery an "abominable crime." Yet and still, he only freed two of his slaves while he was alive, and others were released after he had died.

There was a meeting of delegates from Thirteen Colonies in

the Revolutionary War. There were more than 56 delegates to the Second Continental Congress; these were the Declaration's signatories. The Declaration's goals were to win over foreign allies and proclaim the creation of this new country.

"New Country" may be independent and "new," but America still has its adaptations from slave times. America isn't independent; it depends on the foundations of black people. This country would not be "America" or "The United States" if black people hadn't contributed to the war effort or the Underground Railroad.

You don't just wake up one morning and become a racist. It doesn't matter if there were "early theories of racism," racism has been around ever since the world was created, even in Biblical times. Racism affects how we see the world today; we will never know how racism started or how we can end it. The world we live in is filled with incompetent people. No matter where you look, racism will be the founder of this country.

Independence from the Oxford Dictionary is:
"The fact or state of being independent." Simply means by itself, or lone standing. White people wouldn't have found "America" if it wasn't for black people. Think about that before you upgrade what America's political system looks like. Jefferson only wanted independence for the white man, not for blacks. He claimed America to be adapted to white people but no contribution towards blacks. This nation is NOT independent if you have police officers killing people of a different race.

You are not independent America; you are dependent on race

relations and the political downfall of black people. Think about that.

III

Modern-Day Oppression

Oppression, the term that makes up the United States

15

The Demand of Civil Justice

For many years black people have looked to seek justice over racially profiled crimes committed by someone else, especially among black men. Statistics have shown that black men are 10 times more likely to be accused of a crime they never committed. Formally, sexual assault cases. Black men are the main percentage of rape allegations due to misidentification of black defendants by female white victims. This coincides with murder, drug cases and the release of white exonerees in America. This nation has become the epitome of inequality and fascists government due to incriminating people causing innocent rates among black men in prisons. Racial profiling is a part of some Americans' lives, and for this reason crimes need to be fully examined before arrests are made.

Although people in America have their own doubts about the judicial system, and how corrupt the courts work, racial profiling is the main factor of how sadistic America has become, shackling the duress of black America. The Omaha Race Riots occurred on September 28-29 of 1919. A black man Will Brown was lynched after being accused of "raping"Agnes Loeback a white woman. "On Friday the twenty-sixth, an Omaha Bee headline proclaimed that a "black beast" had assaulted a white girl. Police and detectives combed the vicinity for two hours, joined by four hundred armed men under the leadership of Joseph Loeback (Agnes's brother) and Frank B. Raum. The group included railroad workers who knew Agnes from her job at an eatery (she also worked at a laundry). "A neighbor told the searchers of a "suspicious negro" living in a house at 2418 South Fifth Street with a white woman, Virginia Jones, and a second black man, Henry Johnson."[8]

The audacity of assuming that Will Brown was a "suspicious negro" suggests that every black person is so called "suspicious" simply because we are black. Also, Will Brown had a limp and wasn't able to walk fast, which accounts for why he couldn't have raped Agnes Loeback. She and her family just assumed it was him. These situations are still happening today, whether going to the grocery store and being watched so you won't steal and being pulled over because you had a "broken taillight." All of these coincide with Americas habitual motives, you see a black person, you pull them over because they are "suspicious." Myriads of incidents have happened because America is too blind to sense when a person's life is in danger, money is their only goal. Overall, the famous saying "what goes around comes around" is justifiable, you mistreat us, protests will come.

It's important that this issue is focused on all racial relations in America. From a viewpoint as a biracial young woman,

---

[8] "Lest We Forget: The Lynching of Will Brown, Omaha's 1919 Race Riot." *History Nebraska Blog*, history.nebraska.gov/blog/lest-we-forget-lynching-will-brown-omaha's-1919-race-riot. Accessed 20 May 2022.

it's understandable that individuals say all people of different races are racially profiled. But, in general, think about the struggles black people had to go through to become free (hell and high water). If at the slightest, a slave escaped, their face was on a wanted sign, attached to a tree, labeled as "Missing negro." In the vicinity to see a black man, being burned as white people stand around and laugh as though they made "America great again." Well, America has never been great, what's so great about the death of George Floyd, or Emmett Till, and many other black people. This has lingered for years, but the question remains, what will we do with this unbearable pain. The answer is hidden in plain sight, absolutely nothing. If there isn't a person acceptable in a white person's image, they become outraged, race riots start and black progress declines. In general, the biggest problems faced by black people was and still is the Ku Klux Klan, this white supremacist group specifically targeted black people to scare them after they became free from slavery. "In the summer of 1867, the Klan was structured into the "Invisible Empire of the South" at a convention in Nashville, Tennessee, attended by delegates from former Confederate states. The group was presided over by a grand wizard (Confederate cavalry general Nathan Bedford Forrest is believed to have been the first grand wizard) and a descending hierarchy of grand dragons, grand titans, and grand cyclopes. Dressed in robes and sheets designed to frighten superstitious Blacks and to prevent identification by the occupying federal troops, Klansmen whipped and killed freedmen and their white supporters in nighttime raids."[9]

---

9 "Ku Klux Klan." *Britannica*, www.britannica.com/topic/Ku-Klux-Klan. Accessed 20 May 2022.

There will be no end to racism, this is something you can't fight, even if you defend yourself with the Constitution, racism, racial profiling, and massacres of black people will end this country. Most of the white people back in the day took pleasure of seeing a black person being lynched. The opposing race says that black people don't belong to the United States, as though we are shackled like dogs on a fence. Even though slavery was abolished, America is not the "Land of the Free and Home of the Brave," but rather "Home of the Slaves and the Oppressed." Nevertheless, us a black people welcome in racism, when our people do something, we don't say anything, but rather with a white person, we are subtly quick to judge. We are still the reason we are oppressed and not moving forward. Yes, white people may have taken everything when it came down to our lives, but they have never taken our voice. We cannot be silent about things that matter, we must climb the staircase and bring up those who cannot finish the walk. Press towards the mark of the higher calling and carry on the torch that lights the path. [10]

10

References:

Horowitz, Juliana Menasce, et al. "Race in America 2019." *Pew Research Center*, 9 Apr. 2019, www.pewresearch.org/social-trends/2019/04/09/race-in-america-2019/. Accessed 16 May 2022.

Human Rights. humanrights.gov.au/sites/default/files/whyarepeo-pleracist.pdf. Accessed 18 May 2022.

Jones, Jeffery M., and Camille Lloyd. "Larger Majority Says Racism Against Black People Widespread." *News Gallup*, 23 July 2021, news.gallup.com/poll/352544/larger-majority-says-racism-against-black-people-widespread.aspx. Accessed 16 May 2022.

Nellis, Ashley, Ph.D. "The Color of Justice." *Sentencing Project*, 13 Oct. 2021, www.sentencingproject.org/publications/color-of-justice-racial-and-ethnic-disparity-in-state-prisons/. Accessed 18 May 2022.

"1921 Tulsa Race Massacre." *Tulsa History*, www.tulsahistory.org/exhibit/1921-tulsa-race-massacre/. Accessed 20 May 2022.

Rosin, Hanna. "What 10 Students Learned from Having to Say Their Worst Thoughts on Race out Loud." *Npr Kios*, 16 Mar. 2020, www.npr.org/2020/03/16/814960315/what-10-students-learned-from-having-to-say-their-worst-thoughts-on-race-out-lou?scrlybrkr=d3916a76. Accessed 18 May 2022.

16

Racial Disparities Through the World of Medicine

ave you ever noticed the constant problems black people are facing even today? Especially medical disparities among black people. This is because tests aren't done on black people; it's a closed spectrum of only white people. "Monkey Pox" was the name of the disease going around until people started saying something, and the name was removed. Racial discrimination in hospitals is the third leading factor of racial discrimination in medicine alone. Even throughout medicine, racial discrimination is shown through school systems, housing, etc.

"About three-in-ten Black adults (32%) say they've felt rushed by their health care provider and 29% say they've felt they were treated with less respect than other patients, either recently or in past experiences with doctors and other health care providers. Similarly, 29% say they've felt they've received lower quality medical care at some point; 70% of Black adults say this has *not* happened to them.

Relatively fewer (19%) say they've been looked down on because of their weight or eating habits; 79% say this hasn't happened to them.

Among Black women, 34% say their women's health concerns or symptoms were not taken seriously in interactions with doctors and other health care providers."[11]

Needless to say, the type of care you get can depend on how you are dressed. You see, I can come in the hospital wearing a hoodie and sweatpants and not get proper treatment. But, if I came in looking high class, then of course, I would be feeling like a queen. "Race permeates clinical decision making and treatment in multiple ways, including: (1) **through providers' attitudes and implicit biases, (2) disease stereotyping and clinical nomenclature, and (3) clinical algorithms, tools, and treatment guidelines.**"[12]

Implicit bias, meaning some doctors discriminate on how we are dressed, therefore leading to what kind of healthcare service we receive. Not only so, most clinical studies on done on white people, which doesn't give a clear algorithm for medicine. If medical professionals want to be more inclusive, you have to

---

[11] Funk, Cary. "Black Americans' Views about Health Disparities, Experiences, with

   Healthcare." *Pew Research Center*, 7 Apr. 2022, www.pewresearch.org/-science/

   2022/04/07/

   black-americans-views-about-health-disparities-experiences-with-health-care/.

   Accessed 12 Dec. 2022.

[12] https://www.kff.org/racial-equity-and-health-policy/issue-brief/use-of-r ace-in-clinical-diagnosis-and-decision-making-overview-and-implicati ons/

made medicine attainable, reliable, and effective for all people, no matter the color or content of their character.

Black people are looked down on because of their ethnicity and being. Some doctors refuse to treat patients that are black, it's biased, and states need to train doctors properly that when it comes down to your health, color doesn't matter, you matter, I matter, we all matter. The truth remains that some doctors (not all) only become doctors for money not to treat us with common decency but to push us aside because we have a darker complexion. Research for medicine isn't broad enough; the treatment you give a white person can affect the outcome of a black person. There needs to be more information on racial disparities, how to stop them, and how to drop them. My color shouldn't matter, but how much pain and help I need when it comes to my health.

17

Separate Can Never Be Equal

Supreme Court Landmark Plessy v. Ferguson, ruling that segregation is "separate but equal." Jim Crow moved the reality of this world into hell as though we were dogs. In these pictures you will see below, you tell me if separate is equal.

Police dogs, held by officers, jump at a man with torn trousers during a non-violent demonstration, Birmingham, Alabama, May 3, 1963.

John Lewis, chairman of the Student Nonviolent Coordinating Committee (in the foreground) is being beaten by a state trooper during the march in Selma, Ala., March 7, 1965.

AP

---

[13] Picture on behalf of AARP: Nelms, Cheryl Bond. "Boycotts, Movements and Marches." *AARP*, 9 Feb. 2018,
www.aarp.org/politics-society/history/info-2018/civil-rights-events-fd.html.
Accessed 13 Dec. 2022.

Bloody Sunday attacks. [14]

[14] Picture from: Schwardon, Terry H. "Acts of Violence Are on the Rise, Everywhere."

Progressive Charlestown, 11 Jan. 2020, www.progressive-charlestown.com/

2020/01/americas-dangerous-new-decade.html. Accessed 13 Dec. 2022.

Lynchings arose primarily in the South. [15]

---

[15] "LYNCHINGS IN THE UNITED STATES SINCE 1865." *BlackPast*, www.black-past.org/
special-features/lynchings-united-states-1865/. Accessed 13 Dec. 2022.

Ahmaud Arbery. [16]

Jerome Horton

Trayvon Martin. [17]

[16] Fausset, Richard. "What We Know About the Shooting Death of Ahmaud Arbery."

New York Times, 8 Aug. 2022, www.nytimes.com/article/ ahmaud-arbery-shooting-georgia.html. Accessed 13 Dec. 2022.

[17] "Trayvon Martin Shooting Facts." *CNN*, 14 Feb. 2022, www.cnn.com/2013/06/05/us/ trayvon-martin-shooting-fast-facts/index.html. Accessed 13 Dec. 2022.

Written by CNN Editorial Research

Photograph courtesy of Ben Crump

George Floyd. [18]

All of these, under the face of this nation, were forced into silence. From all of these deaths you see making headlines on national television, to making modern day slavery apart of this nation. You keep us mute, and use every offense against us. But the moment we come together, you're scared. You weren't scared during Bloody Sunday, or lynching black men for no reason, and raping our black women for no reason. When this nation burns to the pits of hell, there will be no more "sorry", because it's too late now.

---

[18] Pos, Mecca. "George Floyd." *MLPS St. Paul,* mspmag.com/arts-and-culture/ george-floyd-remembered/. Accessed 13 Dec. 2022.

18

Impeached

et's get this straight, what would America look like without black people?

America is made up of black soil, black people were put on slave ships, chained together on floorboards, and when an individual had to use the bathroom, they would do their business, and it would flow down on other people.

This is America, the world we live in, where slavery was exemplified as rightful capital involvement. The place you call "America" wouldn't EXIST if black people weren't here.

America is known as a "representative democracy." This simply means we as people are given the ability to choose the representatives for this country. Each citizen is given the eligibility by law to vote (that is, if you are over 18).

This situation still reflects the current election status under political terms. The 1st amendment to the Constitution is "free speech," but when we try to receive justice for our people, we are forced to close our mouths? Every political party has its differences about free speech. In this case, Former President Donald Trump had his views on black people, saying in an interview that he was the best president and has done much for the black community.

"My Admin has done more for the Black Community than any President since Abraham Lincoln."[19]
Trump sounds like a slave owner telling his slaves he's a better Massa. Any man who puts his pants on backward shouldn't be the president of the United States, much less the president of the dog pound.

Seriously, Abraham Lincoln? Lincoln had slaves in his house, and the Emancipation Proclamation didn't help one bit; even though it was passed, it didn't free slaves in the United States. This caused tension for Union states; the Proclamation only freed slaves who were in other states that weren't under Union Control. This meant that slave owners were furious, and they tried to kill their slaves before they could be free. What you do as of now, does affect how your presidency will be, nevertheless, on January 6th, 2021, after Donald Trump lost the presidency, a mob of his supporters attacked the capital. You may think they

---

[19] Kessler, Glenn. "Trump Claims That He Has Done More for the Black Community than
     Any President since Lincoln." *The Washington Post*, 5 June 2020,
     www.washingtonpost.com/politics/2020/06/05/
     trumps-claim-that-hes-done-more-blacks-than-any-president-
     since-lincoln/.
     Accessed 12 Dec. 2022.

only attacked those inside of the building, but it was more than that. Trump supporters hung a noose, and bludgeoned police officers trying to take over the capital.

You would think that idiots such as these would have sense enough to accept that Trump lost, I guess not. How pathetic and stupid can you be to put millions of people in harm just because a narcissistic sociopath lost an election. Not only so, but the fool also started World War III when he told the Proud Boys to "stand back and stand by." Which if you care to notice, he refused to decline any white supremacist group, because Trump classifies as a white supremacy supporter. The only reason he "supports" black people, is because black people turned against him, and he realized that most of his supporters for the election were white. Which, having white only voters say something, if black people refuse to vote for you. Which, we know what would happen if we put a person like Trump up for president. Just one simple word, hell.

"Over the years, Trump has repeatedly egged on white supremacists — who believe that white people are inherently superior — and white nationalists, who want a physical or symbolic white nation, with racist dog whistles. At times, he has even overtly defended them. His affiliation has given a bigger platform to hate-based movements broadly, and they, in turn, have become an indispensable part of his base. The groups became emboldened in the Trump era to make their views more explicit: For instance, during the January 6 insurrection, protesters carried a Confederate Flag into the US Capitol, erected a gallows and noose on the lawn, and evoked a seminal white nationalist text.

Trump has never said explicitly that he supports white nationalism or white supremacy and, as president, repeatedly denounced antisemitism, though he later criticized American Jews for not showing enough gratitude for his support of Israel. (His daughter Ivanka Trump and her husband, Jared Kushner, are Jewish.) On the record, he has disavowed the Ku Klux Klan and its former leader David Duke, who endorsed him for president in 2016, as well as condemned white nationalists, neo-Nazis, white supremacists, and other hate groups. Still, he's continually taken pains not to alienate white extremists, leaving himself room for plausible deniability such that his supporters find no need to question their fealty."[20]

The Insurrection on the capital was modern day slavery. If Trump takes over the United States of America, he will make slavery happen again. This country will never be United because of us. Yes, I mean all of us. Indeed, white people are to blame for slavery, but we as black people are also to blame for the constant oppression. We choose to live under the scales of the white man, we can end it, but we choose not to. We are quick to call out a white man for a crime, but we become mushed mouth about our own people. If Trump chooses to become violent over his actions and pretend to be the victim, so be it. But we can end oppression if we choose to fight against our oppressors. Let Trump be the idiot he was made to be, he just won't be that man here in America

---

[20] Narea, Nicole. "Donald Trump's Long History of Enabling White Supremacy, Explained." *Vox*, 29 Nov. 2022, www.vox.com/policy-and-politics/23484314/ trump-fuentes-ye-dinner-white-nationalism-supremacy?scrlybrkr=d3916a76.
Accessed 19 Jan. 2023.

19

Dear White People, We Are Ending The World

Every single day, someone dies. Either from a gunshot, stabbing, or any other form of violence. Especially upon our black men, our men our targeted for being alive. Humans, normal people living their life. Humans, shooting humans over nothing. We are killing each other, for what? Just so we can be seen on television? What about the little girl who is waiting for her father to read her a bed time story, only to know he's been shot dead in the street. What about the husband who picked up his children from school, only to know he would be shot dead while his kids were in the back seat. How insane can you be, and just ignorant enough to be serious? I can't fathom how many times I've seen a black man either beaten, killed, or lynched for nothing! And you have the audacity to stand up before the people and say "We shall overcome." Overcome what? Overcome the death of innocent black men whose blood still stains the street of Harlem? Then you lie and say "we will rise together." How can that be true if we keep killing each other. The Stock Market will not be the thing that crashes, it will be us. The mother who sheds a tear, one for her daughter who fought off her rapist and was charged with murder. Another tear for her son who was pulled over for a broken taillight and was shot dead in his car, his corpse thrown into the river never to be seen again. Sixty-five more tears for a man calling out to his mother while being beaten. That mother has ran out of tears, each tear she sheds went unnoticed, and you wonder why we stay angry. We have walked across the bridge to find freedom, fought against the deathly shadows of the white man, and called this new nation home. Every single time I see the news, one of my people have died. "Homicide ranks No. 1 as the leading cause of death for African American males ages 1 to 44, and fourth leading cause for African American males for all ages."[21]

The youngest black boy to be killed on death row was only 14, his name was George Stinney. The police made Stinney give a false confession, saying that he murdered two white girls. No, I will not be silenced, you can cut off every piece of me if you want, but I've seen too much to stay quiet. We have fought in the struggle. Who do you think was there when Harlem went up in flames? When they turned the fire houses on? It doesn't matter if you grew up with privilege, it won't matter when you die. We did it matter when you had dogs rip us a part. But, I will say this one thing, don't become scared when we walk together, just because you didnt see the severed head of a black man on massa's doorpost. When we stand, we stand with God, not for you. Change is going to happen, watch out. The Promised Land

---

[21] https://www.gainesville.com/story/special/2020/06/17/homicide-is-leadin g-cause-of-death-of-black-males-age-44-and-younger-in-us/11290078 6/

is where you will find us, but only for those who've been through the struggle, not for those who've stood and watched. They say, never to say goodbye, but rather see you later, I guess that wasn't the case when the black man cried, and you took a part of me.

IV

Face to Face with Black History, Past, Present, and Future

Here you will find pictures of art, culture, and how black people became the movement of America.

20

Gone Missing, the story of James Earl Chaney, Andrew Goodman, and Micheal Schwerner

C haney, Goodman, and Schwerner were arrested in the outer part of Philadelphia on June 21, 1968. As they worked for the COFO, known as the Council of Federated Organizations, this organization united voter activity and registration. Along with other civil rights activists and movements. Their main goal was to help black people vote because they knew we would be prominent in numbers. When it came, it was time to elect a president over the organization; more than 80,000 votes were in favor of Aaron Henry (president of the COFO) and minister Edwin King. The three men, Chaney, Goodman, and Schwerner, are reported missing by their colleagues. Contacting people they could, such as the FBI and others racing against the clock to save them.

These men had been working to register black voters, and the Ku Klux Klan was outraged, resulting in their kidnapping. After the burning of Mt. Zion church, the three men drove to give their condolences to the families. Once they had left the church, they were pulled over by white police officers. Chaney was arrested for supposed speeding. Goodman and Schwerner were imprisoned after suspicions rose, looking to find out if they had burned a church. At 10:30, the three men were released. (Please keep in mind that being out at this time of night was dangerous in this area). While driving down the road on their way to Meridian, they were once again pulled over, this time by more law enforcement and KKK members. They were later taken to a gravel road and murdered. Goodman and Schwerner were only shot once, but Chaney was brutally beaten, castrated, and shot three times.

James Earl Chaney.[22]

James Earl Chaney, a man who went out of his way, with this entire life to make sure that we as black people can vote. This man you see in this picture is my cousin. I never got a chance to see him, because the KKK took him. He never got to tell me the stories of his heroism. It leaves me in tears to know i will never see him.

I'm here on this Earth for a reason. I'm not here to say that you shouldn't live in the United States of America, I'm telling you to look and see what happened. There is no way i can live in this world without knowing how this came about. The United States of America isn't united, it's known as the white man's land, known as the hellhole, the lying dog of a nation, and a scheme to take us. "I'm sick and tired of being sick and tired." I agree Fannie Lou Hamer, i am too. I'm fed up with his country, but, nevertheless, that doesn't mean the fight will not continue. We're coming America, and when we do, there's nothing you can do about it.

---

22 "James Earl Chaney." *Spartacus Educational*, spartacus-educational.com/ USAchaney.htm. Accessed 13 Dec. 2022.

21

Day 1: Memphis Tennessee

This was the most potent uprising Martin Luther King Jr would make, he had made strides along the way, but this is what museums, grandparents, and historians would say. His 2nd most remarkable speech was "I Have Been to the Mountaintop." In his speech, Dr. King gives his prophecy of the "Promised Land." Because Moses disobeyed God, Moses and the Israelites were not allowed to enter the land. A journey that would have only taken 40 days (about 1 and a half months) ended up being 40 years. In his speech, King lets the people know that the time has come to prepare for God's calling to his people. This place was like no other; it would be a place of testimonies of resilience and unity.

This speech became most clear due to the killing of two black sanitation workers who were crushed while on the back of a truck while seeking shelter from the rain. Black people were underpaid through these jobs; they were forced into horrible conditions, often resulting in disease. If a black man had a job, he couldn't afford to miss one day of work, if he did, he would be fired on the spot, and other reprimands would follow. After Jim Crow laws were passed, there was a whole line of rules and regulations black people had to follow. Taking off their hat when talking to a white man, standing up against the wall when a white person was on the same sidewalk. If a black man was caught staring at a white woman, he would be jailed. All these outcomes happened in America's eyes. Therefore, the sanitation workers went on a strike, protesting for the two men who had lost their lives. As Dr. King once said, "Our lives end the moment we become silent about things that matter," which affected black people. Due to the contributions that King made, he became the spotlight, and white people were irate.

In Room 306, MLK shot. As of today, if you visit the museum where the Lorraine Hotel stands, you can see a reef; this is where King was standing on his balcony and shot dead. Below the balcony, you will see two white cars at the time of King's death. It was presumed that MLK was shot from the building across the street from the Hotel.

At the time, the Windsor Hotel in 1945 was an all-white hotel; Memphis being predominantly black, it was dumb to have a whites-only hotel. Because of this, it was later sold to Walter Bailey and his wife, now turned into Lorraine Hotel. It closed and reopened in 1991 as the National Civil Rights Hotel.

It's essential to understand the history left behind; let's ask ourselves. How can we change ourselves for each other and for the more extraordinary beginnings of our history? As MLK is laid to rest, we must be diligent in the crusade of our history; we know the white man wants to take over, but, as a people, we shall overcome.

22

Day 2: Jackson Mississippi

Despite the outrage after King's death, the movement to fight for equal rights amongst black people didn't stop. Black people stood more robust than ever and began to fight back at racial uprising, sparking the voices of many to become heard, seen, and prayed over. One man was Medgar Evers.

Medgar Evers, nonetheless, was a civil rights activist but was also the NAACP's first field secretary. Born on July 2, 1925, in Decatur, Mississippi, Medgar was just one of many who fought for their people. Consequently, before President John F. Kennedy would give his speech to the world, Medgar was shot 150 feet away by Bryon De La Beckwith at his own home. Medgar struggled to get to the steps of his house but later died at the hospital an hour later. Even though his death moved the nation, in his lifetime he was a pioneer, a World War II veteran, and a man who helped integrate Ol' Miss, making James Meridith the first black man to become a student at the racially segregated University.

Fannie Lou Hamer:

This name may sound entirely new to some, but her history is vital to America's political turnover. She was none other than Fannie Lou Hamer. In which she gave her famous quote, "I am sick and tired of being sick and tired."

As a child, Hamer suffered from polio, which causes paralysis in the legs, causing spinal cord damage. As her political uprising began, she was the main target of abuse. Being tortured, beaten in jail, and rushed to the hospital for minor surgery to remove a uterine tumor, a white doctor performed a hysterectomy without Hamer's permission, causing her to have no children. This sort of procedure was torture to black women. Because of this, it was then called the "Mississippi appendectomy." Though Hamer went through much trauma, she never let that belittle her. She went on to become the vice-chair of the Democratic Freedom Party.

There are more people apart from the outstanding success in America, such as Ella Baker, Huey P. Newton, Stokely Carmichael, Eldridge Cleaver, and many more. They never gave up the fight, even if it meant dying for a better tomorrow. We now must take on their legacy, taking not only what was and still is ours but seeing the fruit of black America rise from the oppression of the white man.

23

Day 3: Birmingham Alabama

The city of Birmingham was built after slavery; even though this city peaked with racial tension, black people went on to develop their own industries. A.G. Gaston owned many enterprises and became the black Warren Buffet. Making him the first black millionaire of Alabama. In today's money, Gaston would be worth 135 million dollars, which may not seem a lot to you, but back then, having that type of money said something. It said that you knew how to run things and did it well, especially from a black man. Gaston formed the Boys and Girls Club and owned a hotel where Martin Luther King Jr and other activists would make their war room to prepare for the coming protests. Gaston owned a bottling company, insurance company, banks, and funeral homes. Today, you can see much impact on the work he has done.

Important Headlines During Political and Emotional Tension:

Segregation: Two doctors, Kenneth and Mamie Clark, did

research on four dolls, two being black and two being white. This experimentation would be used in the Supreme Court Case Brown vs. Board of Education; when black people were asked the question, who is the prettiest, and who would you most likely be? Most black people said the white doll was the most stunning and attractive, and they wanted to be that color. Segregation took a toll on how black people looked at themselves; they had to be attentive to the rules of what the white man wanted. Oppression is an objection, but when you get used to living in such conditions, you become dim.

The Cross of the Ku Klux Klan, and the Civil Advancement of the White Man.

The Ku Klux Klan used the cross to separate black and white couples so they wouldn't have children. The cross was used to scare them because they had gotten out of line. To collate along with the Ku Klux Klan, you had some whites who were for black people, and the rest of the whites were just a menace to society.

On August 28, 1955, Emmet Till was murdered. The killing of Emmet Till sparked a movement for black people seeking justice for Emmet, who was tortured and mutilated, shot in the head, and white men threw his body in the Tallahatchie River; they put a cotton gin fan tied with barbed wire around his neck to way Till down so he would sink. These pricks were none other than Roy Bryant and his brother-in-law J.W. Milam. His bloated and beaten body was retrieved from the river. Tills's mother, Mamie, left his casket open for everyone to see what the white men did to her son. On top of this, Eugene "Bull" Conor was chosen as Public Safety Commissioner in 1957, (which is ironic because he didn't give two dimes about Black people's safety). Later, on January 14, 1963, George Wallace

85

was elected governor of Alabama. His preposterous and utterly ignorant motto, "Segregation Today, Segregation Tomorrow, and Segregation Forever." White people were so caught up in their own world of what they wanted that they were willing to die and kill blacks to keep segregation here. With this, white people decided to devise a test to decide what color black you were, it was called the paper brown bag test. This test was to find if a black person was too dark to take part in certain activities.

We must dedicate ourselves to the movement, so our people won't fall to these atrocities. You would think that racism and oppression are gone, and if you think this is true, please seek help because black people are dying under the hand of the white man once again. Open your eyes and see what is happening; your life depends on it. We aren't spring chickens and aren't ready for the stewing pot either.

24

Day 4: Selma Alabama

The day the Earth stood still is the main sight of Bloody Sunday. On January 30, 1972, over 17 million people (about the population of New York) watched this horrific scene of hatred. White supremacists lined up on the other side of the bridge; on their megaphone, the officer warned the black community to go home. Signs of the white man holding up awful racial slurs, saying black people don't belong here. The police began to put on their gas masks, and the officers took off. Black people started running away and were hit with barbed wire baseball bats, batons, and gunshots. Horses ran over them, and white police officers bashed black people's heads in, leaving them with multiple fractures and concussions. Screaming, yelling, and horror rose on black people's faces. Blacks helped anyone they could from being attacked, shielding their parents from being hit, and holding hands while trying to escape this painful massacres. Black people lined up on this bridge to walk for the right to vote.

Marching from Selma to Montgomery took them several days.

The emotional impact of walking across this bridge is deteriorating. John Lewis was brutally beaten, leaving him with speech impediments. Owning the Student Nonviolent Coordination Committee, he became and served as a congressperson in 1982 until the day he died. He was fighting the battle for social and civil rights. When MLK was shot in 1968, John Lewis fought as a foot soldier and became one of the civil rights movement's heroes. John Lewis returned home to Atlanta and ran for city council, and he won on the spot. John Lewis was right along with his people, running the same race and jumping the same hurdles.

So, my colleagues and I decided to remember what that day was about. We took a bus to Selma. On our way, we watched the movie, Selma; in this movie, we watched the Bloody Sunday scene with emotion; we needed to cross this bridge. We stood, and sentiment began to take over; as we stood together praying, we began to walk. Remembering the bloody battle, we knew that crossing this bridge would bring different emotions to our faces but walking against what the world says brings about more than a motive; it brings victory. Victory to see how far we have come.

While walking on the bridge, 3/4 of the way, we saw the Alabama River; this river is the 2nd most heart-wrenching thing to see. Many black people were thrown over the bridge and into the water, never to be recovered.

The Alabama River. Black people were thrown into this river; their bodies were never recovered.

At the end of the walk, we all saw the Civil Rights Trail. This trail, before the time of its naming, was a place where white people sold enslaved people. They would take black people like herds of cattle and bring them to the trail. They also had auction blocks, in which they would put black men on the steps, looking to see which black man was the strongest to do the white man's work.

Civil Rights Trail, enslaved black men were sold here.

91

The Bridge:

The Edmund Pettus Bridge was named after a Ku Klux Klan member. They want to make it the John Lewis Bridge, but why is it still called this? Many black people don't want the name changed because Bloody Sunday happened on that bridge. It's awful to know that a bridge such as this still is the sight of the painful and emotional turmoil for Alabama.

DAY 4: SELMA ALABAMA

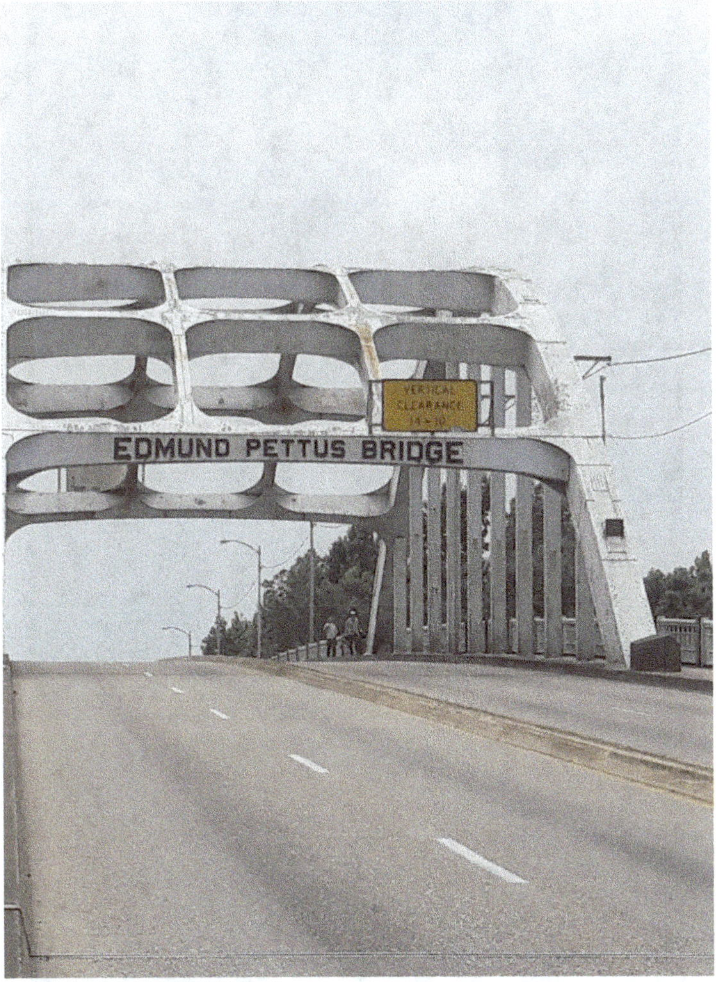

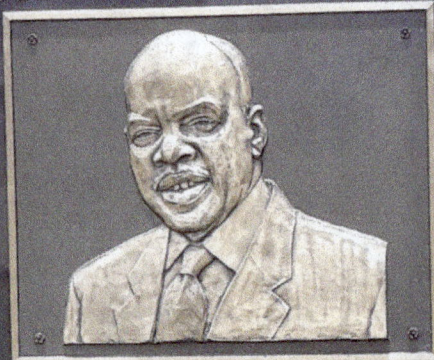

94

Dr. Martin Luther King
&
Coretta Scott King
Partners in Marriage and Movement

Selma to Montgomery | March 1965

*Love is the Bedrock
of Justice & Freedom*
Presented by
Founders of North Star Beloved Community
Hank & Rose Sanders

25

Why was the Civil Rights Movement Important?

America, the nation that is supposedly "under God." It's one thing to be United, and one to be separate. United means "together," henceforth "United States of America."

But what is a nation that is divided by color? Truth is, it's not a nation, it's just another place on the globe that has no meaning. Before the Civil Rights Movement began, black people were fed up with the constant dehumanization they were facing. Nevertheless, if you saw a person's mutilated body hanging from a tree for no reason, you'd be fed up too. That is why people such as Claudette Colvin, 14, was the first young girl to sit at the front of the bus. Most don't know about her because she was dark color, and pregnant. They refused to televise what she had done). JoAnn Robinson was the founder of the Montgomery Bus Boycott, and organizing it to have multiple black leaders who were a part of this. Before getting into the people who helped organize this powerful movement, we need to examine how it started and the prevalence of this movement.

How did the Civil Rights Movement begin?

The civil rights movement became prevalent after the 1954 Supreme Court decision Brown vs. Board of Education, this decision overturned desegregation of schools across the entire nation. But, rather in the South, they were slow to follow the decision and the registration of new black students often broke out into whites engaging in violence. In 1955, Rosa Parks refused to give up her seat, she was later arrested for disorderly conduct and booked at the City of Montgomery Police Department. Thereafter, in December of 1955, this situation ignited the Montgomery Bus Boycott, in which people would not take public transportation to work but walk as a peaceful protest. Although the Boycott was organized by women, Dr. Martin Luther King Jr was the leader due to discrimination against women, and they were not able to run the protests. With the attempts to end desegregation of public transit and in schools, copious amounts of protests began to spew in the country. In 1960, sit-ins and rallies began by SNCC, SCLC, and CORE began to bring an to end discrimination.

What achievements did the Civil Rights Movement receive?

These protests had media outlets everywhere from aboard, and with negotiation from Dr. King and help from the Civil Rights Movement, President Lyndon B. Johnson passed the Civil Rights Act of 1964, and the Voting Rights Act of 1965. Even though laws were being passed to help get rid of modern-day slavery, black people were infuriated with how slow things were being achieved. This is how the Black Power Movement came into play. These non-violent protests proved that violence is not always the answer. Martin Luther King Jr exemplified this as he walked from Selma to Montgomery Alabama, though he

97

was not there for the Bloody Sunday attacks, he knew the pain they went through on that bridge. He saw the torment and the evils of the white man, because the American flag had failed to protect them. Militant advice was out of the picture, they had to take matters into their own hands, and they did just that.

Were there consequences of the Civil Rights Movement.

We all know that with victory comes consequences and conflict. The same opposing argument happened, there was still injustice. No matter how hard you fight, there's going to be injustice everywhere. Even after Dr. King's assassination in 1968, riots broke, and black people were brutally beaten. In some countries, they went against the law and still had poll taxes. If the law is implemented and passed, you can't make people follow the law, they will break it. That is what white people did, as a conglomerate they made sure that whatever we tried to do, we failed. After peaceful protests and exercising their rights, black people were still put down because of it. These initially aren't consequences, but they are still the effects which we leave behind.

Overall, the Civil Rights Movement was indeed successful. They broke patterns of segregation and inequality. They were able to desegregate school districts and way of interstate travel. Achieving what they genuinely wanted, freedom. But, as of today we do not have freedom, we need to walk in the footsteps Dr. King laid out so we can see what America truly is. Let it be known that one day, all will be free.

26

National Voting Rights Museum and Institute

H ere you will find the timeline of which things happened in the United States. Foot Soldiers and Civil Rights members founded this museum after the Bloody Sunday attack, this was founded in 1991.

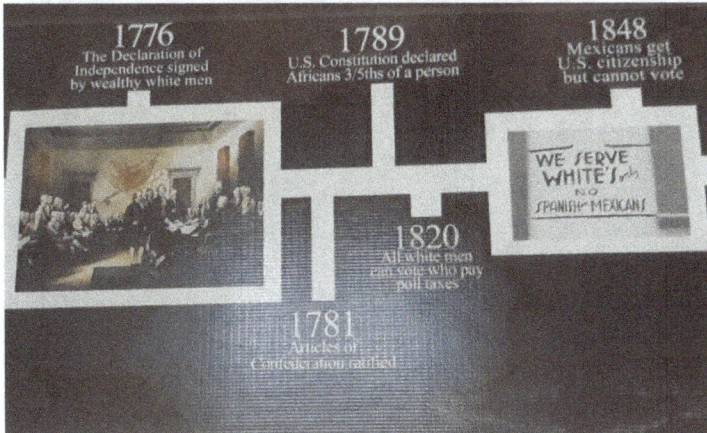

1855
John Langston
(Town Clerk, Brownhelm, OH)
1st black elected official

1865
December 6th
the 13th Amendment
legally ends slavery

1861
April 12th
the Civil War begins

1865 – 1877
Reconstruction Era

1870
February 3rd
15th Amendment enacted -
Black men have the
constitutional
right to vote

Joseph Rainey elected as
first black man to Congress

1866
Civil Rights Act granted
citizenship to
native born Americans
except "Indians"

1882
The Chinese Exclusion Act
keeps Chinese Americans
from citizenship and voting
CONSTITUTION
OF THE
STATE OF ALABAMA
1916
February 3rd
Jeanette Rankin -
First woman
elected to Congress
1901
Alabama Constitution was created to keep
blacks and poor whites from unifying
underminding their right to vote

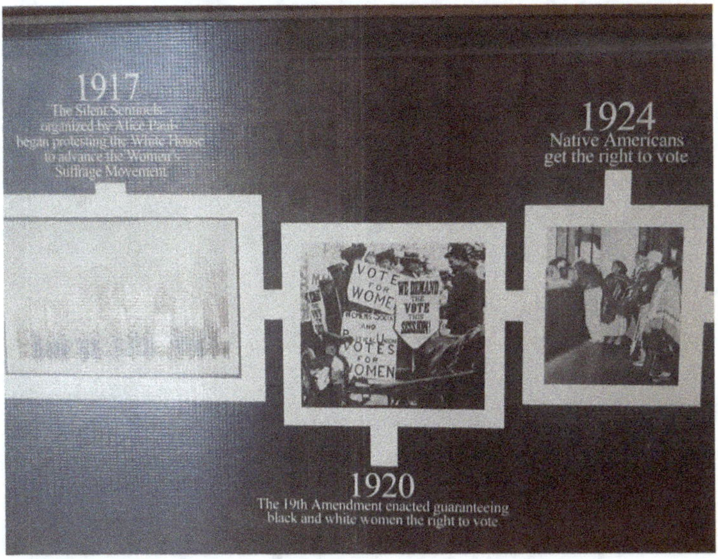
1917
The Silent Sentinels
organized by Alice Paul
began protesting the White House
to advance the Women's
Suffrage Movement
VOTE FOR WOMEN
WE DEMAND THE VOTE THIS SESSION
VOTES FOR WOMEN
1924
Native Americans
get the right to vote
1920
The 19th Amendment enacted guaranteeing
black and white women the right to vote

1933
C.J. Adams and others organize
the Dallas County Voters League
VOTE
1928
Samuel Boynton
comes to Selma
1954
Brown vs. Board
of Education of
Topeka Supreme
Court decision

1955
August 28th
Emmett Till
murdered by white men
in Money, MS
1963
May - Sam Boynton dies
and first mass meeting
at Tabernacle is held
1962
Bernard Lafayette
of S.N.C.C.
arrives in Selma
1963
Marie Foster begins
Citizenship Classes
September 15th
16th Street Baptist Church
Killings

1964
Rev. F. D. Reese
signs the letter
from the Courageous 8
from the Dallas Co.
Voter's League inviting
Dr. Martin Luther King, Jr. to Selma

1964
June 21st
Schwerner, Goodman, and Chaney
killed in Philadelphia, MS
while registering people to vote

1964
December - S.C.L.C. workers and
students break the injunction barring 3 or
more Blacks from assembling together

1966
First Black Mayor elected
to a U.S. city
Robert C. Henry of Springfield, OH

1971
The 26th Amendment
gives 18-year-olds
the right to vote

1966
Lowndes County
Freedom Organization
(a.k.a the original
Black Panther Party)
founded by
Stokely Carmichael
and other young civil
rights workers

1967
August 31st - Thurgood Marshall
became the 1st African American
U. S. Supreme Court Justice

2000
First Black Mayor of Selma
James Perkins

2004
Hip Hop artists and activists
like P. Diddy, Russell Simmons, T.I.
and Queen Latifah
mobilized youth to vote in
the presidential elections of 2000, 04, and 08

1994
April 27th South African
Apartheid ends -
Leaders inspired
by American
Voting Rights Movement

2003
The National Hip Hop
Political Convention founded

2008
November 4th
President Barack Obama elected
the 44th President of
the United States of America

27

We Are The Movement

My ancestors fought for our freedom from lynchings, beatings, and mobs; they did it not for themselves but for you. Praying that you wouldn't go through the same experience they had. They wanted you to become a part of America, but also, they wanted you to know that if you are tired of running, remember who you are running for and why. Never forget that you are the generation that will carry the baton. Our ancestors are gone, but we must never forget how they paved the way for us. We are the movement.

It's horrible to know that we live in a country like America. I'm ashamed to see how the place I have always called home is now a conglomerate joint of radicalized damage to the black man. I'm not afraid to say, America is the home of murdering innocent black men. This nation is falling into a plateau of ignorant people. We associate black people as "the slaves," but rather, they were enslaved, they were never slaves. America, you took that from them and led to diseases like the KKK. I hope you realize what you have done. Just remember, as the great Maya Angelou said, "You may shoot me with your words, you may cut me with your eyes, you may kill me with your hatefulness, but still, like air, I'll rise!"

V

Award Winning Speeches

Dedicated to the black people of this nation.

28

Freedom Rider

Nights and days get nearer, and the war cry of black people lingers in the midnight rain. Freedom glows in the eyes of those who will never see it. As we know, the killing of black people is returning to what it once was. We say the pledge of Allegiance with such pride, even though the person who made it was an enslaver. The words are claiming America to be "The land of the free, and the home of the Brave," but look around you, America is still "Home of the Slaves, and the Oppressed." The very same place you sit in this very nation, was built upon white supremacy. Portuguese traders had brought a myriad of enslaved people from Africa to Europe. Consequently, eighty-two years later, Spanish prospectors brought the enslaved Africans to different settlements that would become the United States. So, how can you call this place America if all men aren't created equal, and the founders of this nation were enslavers? You put us to work because you wanted to get rid of the tedious labor and put it upon people you knew would be something more than just a beggar on the street. The same people claimed us as property, hid us from books, interaction with the world, and reprimanded us from learning because they knew we would be dangerous. 90% of schools tutor students about the Holocaust, World War II, and the Emancipation Proclamation. Well, I got news for you, the Emancipation Proclamation did not free slaves; there were still 3.4 million enslaved people that weren't aware of their freedom. Do you call that social justice? Did you understand that the 13th Amendment did not free slaves? It reads, "Neither slavery nor involuntary servitude, except as a punishment for the crime of which the party shall have duly convicted, shall exist within the United States."

What about the countless men you destroyed under oath, George Smith, who was accused of raping a five- year-old white girl Lizzie Yates. Years later, she had stated that George never raped her! Emmett Till was tortured and lynched for offending a white woman. Trayvon Martin was shot by a man who called him "a real suspicious guy" just because he was black. Michael Brown was hit by a white police officer. Will Brown was lynched for raping a white woman. James Craig Anderson was severely beaten and intentionally ran over by a truck by a group of white teenagers; Eric Garner was put into a chokehold by a white police officer killing him. George Floyd, who was arrested by Derek Chauvin, had his knee on Floyd's neck. These are the people you killed and stood right there and laughed, ignoring the cry of innocent black men. You say, "Liberty and Justice for all," if it were true, why did we have Jim Crow, slave codes, black codes, Ku Klux Klan, and Gun Control Acts? And the Ku Klux Klan is still rampant in this country we call America; now, do you call that social justice? And please, understand white people aren't white; they are pale pink, they don't own America, they live in it just like I do.

And as Martin Luther King once said, "If the cruelties of slavery could not stop us, the opposition we now face will surely fail." Whatever happens in the world better be the business of all of us. Because I, Too, Am AMERICA.

29

I Too Have a Dream Dr. King

It was a dark, humid summer's night; all my family gathered outside in secret to remember a loved one; my brother was lynched. His name was Emmett Till. As we buried him, I stood there, my virtue gone. Massa was in the house asleep.

"My baby, my sweet baby. Jesus, take him on; my son was a good boy, but I know he's no longer hurting; he's at peace." Mama kissed his body, and they covered him.

I looked at the ground where he was. Anger lifted in my veins, and I began to say.

One day my people will come together and stand forth above the heavens. I dream that day, my people will rise from their fleshly desires and look into the eyes of the white man and say, "I will not be moved!" You can spit on me, kick me, rock me, and call me any name that pleases you, but I am a member of this country. I am no negro, I am no lying dog, I am no boy, I am no rapist, I am nothing you say. I will not take my hat off to any white man, I will not bow down to you, I am not the maid to your masa, I am a dignified person. I, too, dream that one day the whip that beat me will burn on the face of this country. I, too, have a dream that my people will seek God's face, turn from their wicked ways, and he will hear a cry from heaven, and he will heal our land. I, too, dream that my children will become the better face of America and beat the wrongdoing. When the clock strikes midnight, he will be like a theft in the night, to steal, kill, and destroy. But under the face of the sun, all people, no matter the color, shall be that of a rising river, mighty in battle. When the undertaker had come to his mom, he said "it is now time to view the body." She looked down at her baby and the tears rolled, the next day was the funeral. The undertaker informs me of having a closed casket because you could see what they had done to my child, they had lynched my son due to the color of his skin. I told them "NO, NOT SO, I want everyone, everyone, to see the racism that goes on in this country, and what they did to my child, and he was only 14 years old, because of the color of his skin. They killed my baby, they lied on my baby, and took my baby's life, THE CASKET WILL NOT BE CLOSED. And if I live, I want everybody to understand, because racism is on the move as I speak. I want everyone to know, that Black Lives Matter. "Until justice rolls down like water and righteousness like a mighty stream." We are not slain, we are not lame, we are the blackness. The whip that our Massa's use will be the same whip they will cry out to when all hell breaks loose. Every valley shall be exalted, and every mountain and hill brought low; The crooked places shall be made straight and the rough places smooth; The glory of the LORD shall be revealed, and all flesh shall see it together; For the mouth of the LORD has spoken." I have the same dream, Dr. King; I have that dream; I am the dream because I live the dream. I dream of that world because it shall be divine.

30

To Hell and Back

"Being a Negro in America means trying to smile when you want to cry. It means trying to hold on to physical life amid psychological death. It means the pain of watching your children grow up with clouds of inferiority in their mental skies. It means having your legs cut off, and then being condemned for being a cripple. It means seeing your mother and father spiritually murdered by the slings and arrows of daily exploitation, and then being hated for being an orphan." -Quote by Dr. Martin Luther King Jr.

Society is made up of words, it's our daily communication, but this word grasps the attention of many. A country divided by such a strong word, that it keeps people from seeing what truly is of America. A world so divided by a word that every single news headline talks about it. Race, a four letter word that describes this nation as a whole. Not only does society keep us mute from advocating for equality, it tells us that we don't belong. But, one man would change that and make the Earth stand still.

On December 18, 2016 Former Quarterback for San Francisco 49ers Colin Kaepernick kneeled during the National Anthem. This situation sparked outrage among military families, and white people. Becoming seen throughout the world, not just more than once, but over 50 million times. So, the question is posed as follows, how can we make America unified as one flesh, and end the cycle of racial inequality. But, before we discuss a solution, we need to understand the issue.

The overall question given by sportjournal.com states that "How did the NFL respond to the Colin Kaepernick protests in 2016-2017 and how does that compare to the NFL's reaction to current athlete protests during the BLM movement of 2020?" After his kneeling, the NFL condemned Kaepernick of his actions and told him that it was disrespectful to military service. He stated in an interview with the NFL saying that: "I am not going to stand up to show pride in a flag for a country that oppresses black people and people of color. To me, this is bigger than football and it would be selfish on my part to look the other way."[23]

Understand this, the National Anthem wasn't meant for black people, it was meant for the white man. I am not going to stand

---

[23] Donahue, Ben. "How the NFL Responded to the Colin Kaepernick Protests in
2016-2017 and How the League Responded to Athlete Protests during the Black
Lives Matter Movement of 2020: A Sport Study, Social Phenomenological
Approach." *Sports Journal*, thesportjournal.org/article/
how-the-nfl-responded-to-the-colin-kaepernick-protests-in-2016-2017-and-how-the-l
eague-responded-to-athlete-protests-during-the-black-lives-matter-movement-of-202
0-a-sport-study-social-phenomenologi/. Accessed 19 Jan. 2023.

up for a malicious scam that gave me nothing. The American Dream, The Declaration of Independence, and the National Anthem were ALL MADE BY SLAVE OWNERS.

- Francis Scott Key, a slave owner, an Attorney of DC, which he supported strict slave laws. Even though he stated "The land of the Free, and the home of the brave."
   - Thomas Jefferson, owned the most slaves out of any US president (owning 600). "We hold these truths to be self-evident, that all men are created equal, that among these are life Liberty and the pursuit of happiness." "Jefferson owned over 600 enslaved people during his lifetime."[24]

Not only are these problems self evident, but this same exact example deals with the assassination of President John F. Kennedy, he was shot and killed because of Martin Luther King Jr, he was for the black people and America could not stand it. To prove this historynewsnetwork.org, in a book called "In Cold Blood", written by Dr. Jospeh's Satten states that: "In attempting to assess the criminal responsibility of murderers, the law tries to divide them (as it does all offenders) into two groups, the 'sane' and the 'insane'. The sane murderer is thought of as acting upon rational motives that can be understood, though condemned, and the insane one as being driven by irrational senseless motives."[25]

---

[24] "Slavery FAQ's- Property." *Monticello*, www.monticello.org/slavery/slavery-faqs/
   property/. Accessed 19 Jan. 2023.

[25] Ayton, Mel. "Lee Harvey Oswald's Motives." *History News Network*,
   historynewsnetwork.org/article/23430. Accessed 19 Jan. 2023.

Through the bloody horrors black people have seen through slavery, all of the slave owners who committed murder, none of them were held accountable for their crimes. Simply because of disparate treatment and nationalism. Through the political actions of government ties, we were supposed to receive "Life Liberty and the Pursuit of Happiness," what a crock of bull! Were we happy when you tied us to trees and beat the skin off our backs? Were we happy when we had our children and you took them away from us? Raped us, threw us overboard, you think this is happiness? And at least 75% of the rapes on our black women you left a child, that is some of the reason why black women were killed, and if the child was of light color you kept, and let others raise him or her, particularly a girl. EJI.org states that "Enslaved Black women had no legal means to resist or protect themselves from sexual assault by white slaveowners."[26]

America laughs at the black man because of our dark complexion, well, how about you take a look in the mirror too, because you white people are black. White wasn't a popularized word until 1775; it was used as a weapon of white supremacy to demonize and uplift white people. Instead, you are pale pink, you aren't the color of snow, or paper. It it because of the melanin in your skin that makes you look physically different from me. But do not get the big head because of the color of your skin, remember now, I'm as light as some of you, we come in all colors, you just come in one, pale pink.

---

[26] "Sexual Violence Targeting Black Women." *EJI*, eji.org/report/ reconstruction-in-america/the-danger-of-freedom/sidebar/ sexual-violence-targeting-black-women/. Accessed 19 Jan. 2023.

Supreme Court Landmark Plessy v. Ferguson, ruling that segregation is "separate but equal." How can separate be equal? Jim Crow moved the reality of this world into hell as though we were dogs. All of these, under the face of this nation, were forced into silence. From all of these deaths you see making headlines on national television, to making modern day slavery apart of this nation. You keep us mute, and use every offense against us. But the moment we come together, you're scared. You weren't scared during Bloody Sunday, or lynching black men for no reason, and raping our black women for no reason.

America laughed at Will Brown when he was burned,
   You didn't hear the cry of Emmett Till when we was brutally tortured, and thrown in the Tallahatchie River, and right here in Omaha Nebraska, Vivian Strong, who was 14 years old, was shot in the head and killed without warning by James Loder. Now you tell me, what's fair about that?

You didn't hear the cry of George Floyd, when Derek Chauvin put his knee on Floyd's neck, You, America, didn't hear Daunte Wright, Andre Hill, Manuel Ellis, Breonna Taylor, Atatiana Jefferson, Stephon Clark, Botham Jean, Alton Sterling, Freddie Gray, Eric Garner, Tamir Rice, Micheal Brown, and my cousin, James Earl Chaney who died at the hands of pale pink people. No one, and I repeat no one was charged with his murder, and two of his co workers were pale pink, their names were Andrew Goodman, and Micheal Schwerner. So, HOW DARE YOU, THINK THAT YOU ARE BETTER THAN ME, JUST BECAUSE OF THE COLOR OF YOUR SKIN.
They died under your eyes, but you did nothing. This is the place we live in, the area that we call home. We aren't together as one,

but your flesh under one individual. The wounds and scars my people went through just to get by should never EVER happen. If I remember correctly, God made man out of the richest soil which was reddish-black dirt, so, just bare with me a minute, how do you get white from black dirt? Just a question I'd like for you to ponder. And trust me when I tell you, if I cut you, you will not bleed white blood, your blood is red, just like mine.

So, with all of the problems we discussed, how can we make America unified? The answer is simple, we can't. As a young black girl, Colin Kaepernick kneeling was important to me because he gave those who were voiceless a voice. To finally stand up for what's right. But, America will never be unified because there will always be racism. There is no way to end this cycle, no law, no government ruling or court decision.

So, if it means that I have to get down one knee to justify what this nation did to my people. It doesn't mean I'm being disrespectful, it means that I am the blackness. Because sometimes you have to get down on one knee in order to finish the race. Remember, the rabbit was the fastest but the tortoise won the race. You cannot win the race looking behind you.

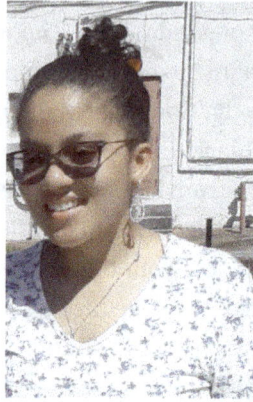

About the Author

Kaleciana Gabrielle Torjai Perry is 15 years old and attends Omaha Central High School, currently a sophomore. Writing has been an interest to her ever since she was 11 years old. The more she learned about her brother who was autistic, the more she wanted to write. She is blessed and the favor of God is upon her. She is a public speaker for Civil Rights and has always said she wants to be a Civil Rights Attorney. Her awards vary in many amounts; she's on the honor roll, which she has been on for 4 years. She was inducted into the Tri-M Music Honor Society on January 26, 2023, also for 2 straight years she has held her 1st place spot in the "Living the Dream Competition." Her award-winning speeches include, "Freedom Rider," "I too have a Dream Dr. King," and, "To Hell and Back," and many others. Overall, Kaleciana has proven her fight in the struggle for a better tomorrow and becoming the face of the upcoming generation.

www.ingramcontent.com/pod-product-compliance
Lightning Source LLC
LaVergne TN
LVHW021122080426
835513LV00011B/1195

9 781960 065889